LET'S LEARN
MAJOR DOMAINS OF THE EARTH

Shaheera Aziz

notionpress.com

INDIA • SINGAPORE • MALAYSIA

ISBN 979-8-89277-775-9

I will teach you all major domains of the earth

WHAT ARE
DOMAINS??

I love playing on the beach.

The cool breeze on my face, the sand under my feet, waterflowing in beautiful waves.

Imagine you are walking on a beach and you feel the sand beneath you. You feel the cool ocean breeze on your face as well as the water of the waves crashing on your feet. Sand here is the Lithosphere, the water is the Hydrosphere and the coolbreeze is the Atmosphere. To summarise, the major domains are the Lithosphere, Hydrosphere, Atmosphere and Biosphere.

Atmosphere

Hydrosphere

Lithosphere

Lithosphere is the solid portion of the earth

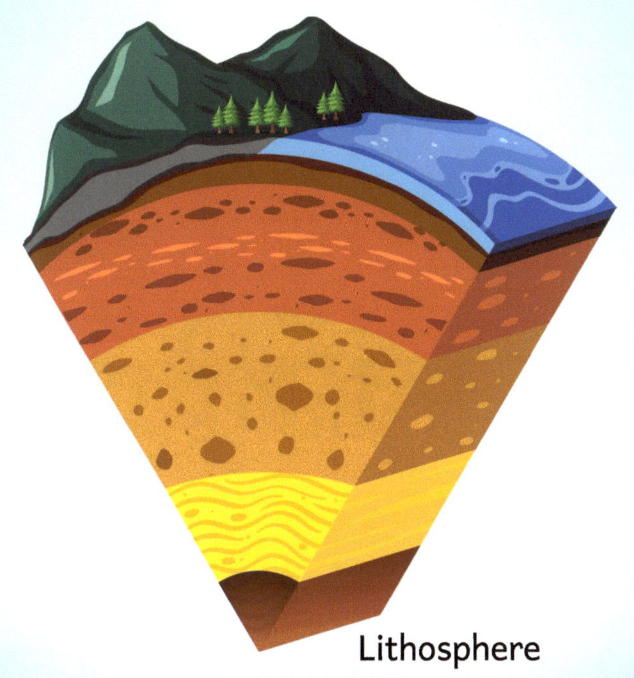

Lithosphere

Atmosphere is the gaseous layers that surrounds the earth.

The air all around us is the Atmosphere

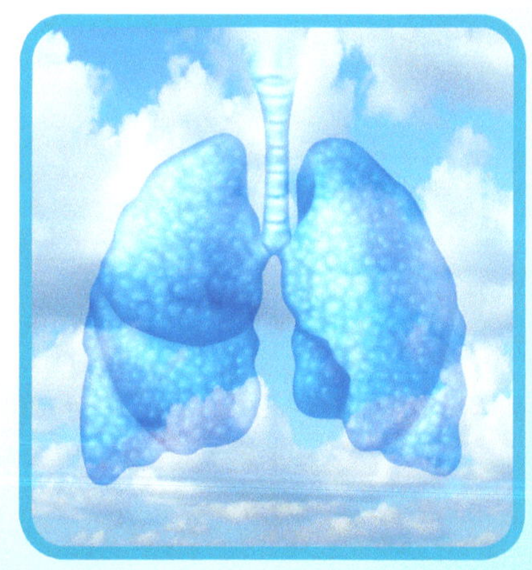

Hydropshere is the part
where water covers a very big
area of the earth's surface.

The water that sorrounds the earth
is Hydrosphere.

Biosphere is the narrow zone where we find land, water and air together which contain all forms of life.

Land, water, air and life together is Biosphere.

Oh wow! I
play, dance, sing and
study on
Lithosphere.

Lithosphere

The solid portion of the earth is called Lithosphere. It comprises of the rocks of the earth's crust and the thin layers of soil the contain nutrient elements which sustain organisms. There are two main divisions of the earth's surface. The large landmasses are known as continents and the huge water bodies are called ocean basins. All the oceans of the world are connected with one another.

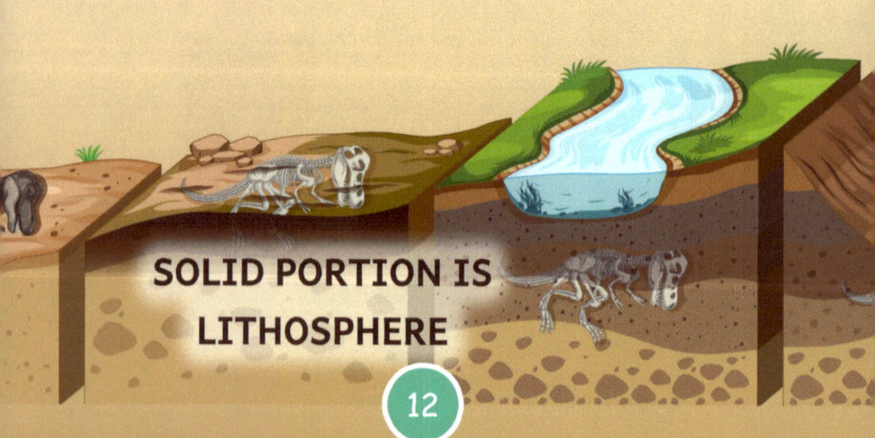

The level of sea water remains the same everywhere. Elevation of land is measured from the level of sea which is taken as zero. The continents are the solid land masses that come under Lithosphere.

Continents

There are seven major continents. They are separated by large water bodies. These continents are–Asia, Europe, Africa, North America, South America, Australia and Antartica.

1. Asia

Asia is the largest continent. It covers about one-third of total land area earth. The continent lies in Eastern Hemisphere. Tropic of cancer passes throughout this continent. Asia is separated from Europe by the Ural mountains on the west combined with landmass are called Eurasia.

2. Europe

Europe is a lot more modest than Asia deceiving the west of Asia. The Arctic Circle goes through it. Its three sides are limited by water bodies. Europe is smaller than Asia.

3. Africa

Africa is the second largest continent after Asia. The equator runs almost through the middle of the continent. A large part of Africa lies in the Northern Hemisphere. You will find that it is only continent through which the Tropic of Cancer, the Equator and the the Tropic of Capricorn pass.

4. North America

North America is the third largest continent of world. It is linked to South by a very narrow strip land called Isthmus Panama. The continent lies completely in Northern and Western Hemisphere. Three oceans surround the continent.

5. South America

South America lies mostly in the Sourthern Hemisphere. Which two oceans sorround it on east and west? The Andes, world's longest mountain range, runs through its length from north to south. South America has worlds largest river, Amazon.

6. Australia

Australia is the smallest continent that lies in the Southern Hemisphere. It is also known as Oceania which is an island continent surrounded by the Indian and Pacific oceans. It is known for its, the Great Barrier Reef, a vast interior desert wilderness called the Outback and unique animal species like kangaroos and duck billed platypuses which are foud no where else.

7. Antartica

Antarctica is the southernmost continent and site of the South Pole, it is a virtually uninhabited and is in the completely ice-covered land. Australia and Antarctica entirely lie in the southern hemisphere.

NOW I KNOW,
WE LIVE ON LITHOSPHERE.

Hydrosphere

Hydrosphere is a domain that contains water or water bodies. If we take the earth into consideration. Only 1/4th(29%)of the earth is covered in soil/land while the rest 3/4th(71%) portion is covered in water.97% of the earth's water is found in oceans and is not suitable for use as it is saltwater.

About the Oceans

Oceans cover a large part of the globe. There are four primary oceans on Earth, which are Pacific Ocean, Atlantic Ocean, Indian Ocean and Arctic Ocean.
The Arctic is a polar region located in the northernmost part of the Earth. It connects to the Pacific Ocean through a Strait known as Bering Strait that passes through Russia and America.
The 'S'shaped region between Europe, America and Africa is the Atlantic Ocean.

Hydrosphere

The Pacific Ocean extends from the Arctic Ocean in the north to the Southern Ocean in the south. The Pacific Ocean is circular in shape and along the Pacific Ocean, there is a "Ring of Fire' meaning it's an active volcanic belt. Now, the Indian Ocean extends from South Asia to Australia as well as Africa. It has gained a uniqueness due to its wind currents.

Atmosphere

The atmosphere is a domain that consists of layers which are the troposphere, stratosphere, thermosphere and mesosphere as well as exosphere. Lifeform sustains on troposphere which is the first layer of the atmosphere. The density of atmosphere is maximum at sea level and decreases with increasing height.

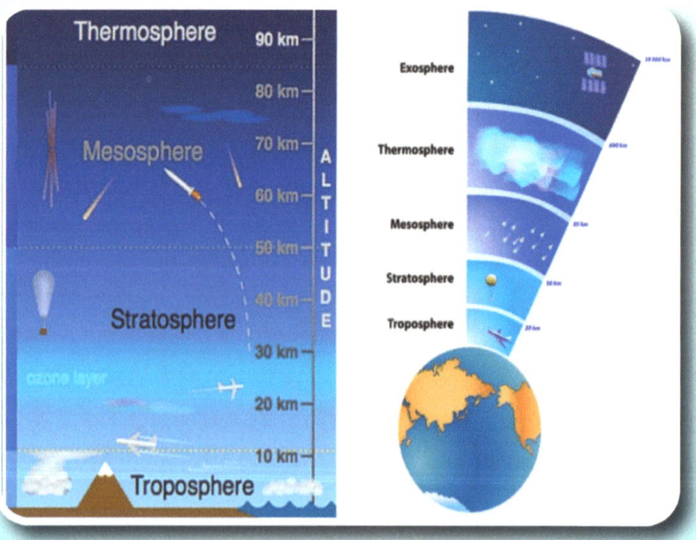

The atmosphere consists of 78% Nitrogen, 21% oxygen and other gases like Argon, Carbon dioxide as well as some other gases comprise 1% of the volume.

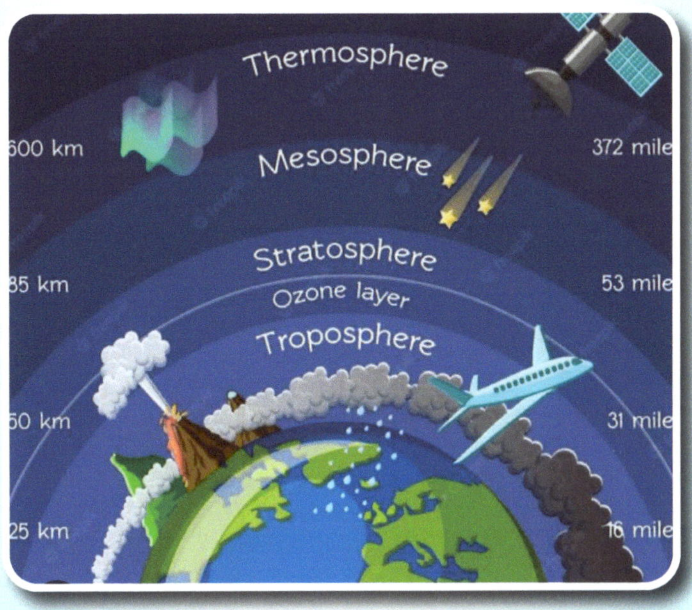

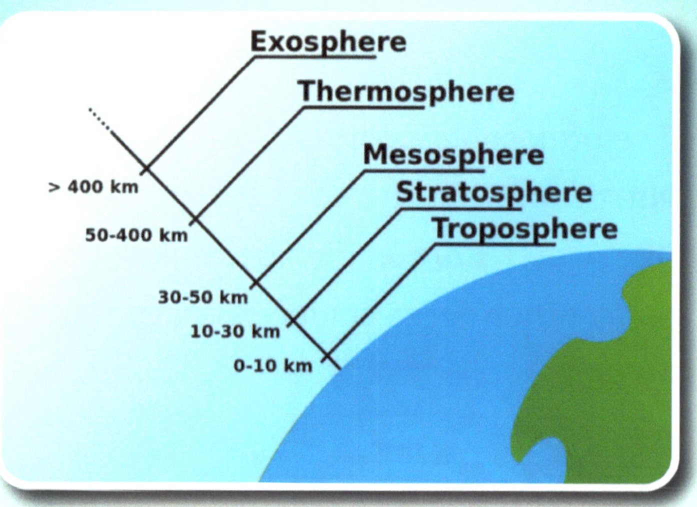

Exosphere
Thermosphere
Mesosphere
Stratosphere
Troposphere
> 400 km
50-400 km
30-50 km
10-30 km
0-10 km

LET ME TAKE A DEEP BREATH AND FEEL THE AIR.

What Is Biosphere?

The biosphere is made up of the Earth where life exists-all ecosystems. The biosphere extends from the deepest root systems of trees, to the dark environments of ocean trenches, to lush rain forests, high mountain tops and transition zones like this one where ocean and terrestrial ecosystems meet.

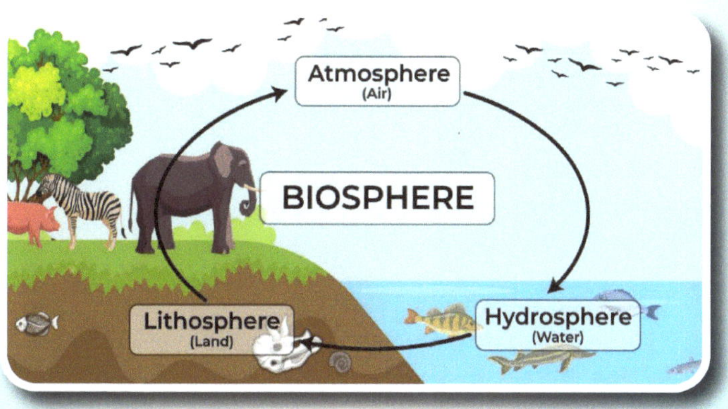

The biosphere is the region of the earth where life can exist and grow. It is the part of the planet where life is capable of existence . The biosphere is also known as the Ecosphere, which means the constitution of all the ecosystems exists worldwide.

It is an open system that uses photosynthesis to absorb solar energy at a rate of about 130 Terawatts per year. The system is self-regulating and nearly in energy equilibrium.

The biosphere, according to the broad sense of physiology, is the ecological system that includes all living creatures and their relationships including their interactions with the lithosphere, geospheres, hydrosphere and atmosphere.

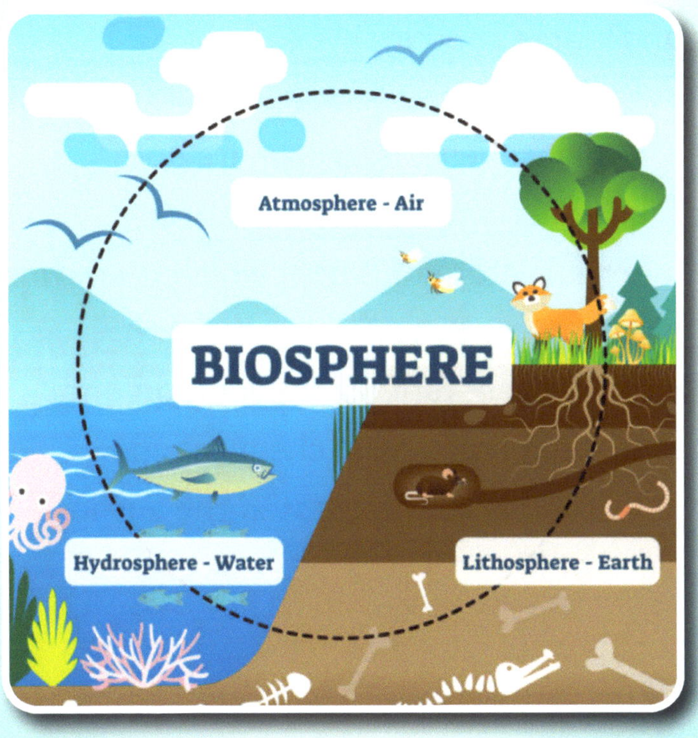

What are biosphere and its Components?

Earth was a barren planet with shallow seas and a thin band of gases before life appeared there. These gases were primarily Carbon dioxide, Carbon monoxide, Nitrogen, Hydrogen sulfide and water vapour.

The lithosphere, hydrosphere and atmosphere make up this entirely inorganic state of Earth, which is known as the geosphere. The early Earth received constant solar radiation and over million of years, chemical and physical processes created the earliest signs of life.

Components of Biosphere

It is made up of the parts of the earth where life exists. Not only humans exist but also plants and animal life. It includes deep forests to grassland from ocean to rain forests from mountains to plains. Scientists have described the place where life exists on earth that is biosphere as a combination of the lithosphere, atmosphere and hydrosphere.

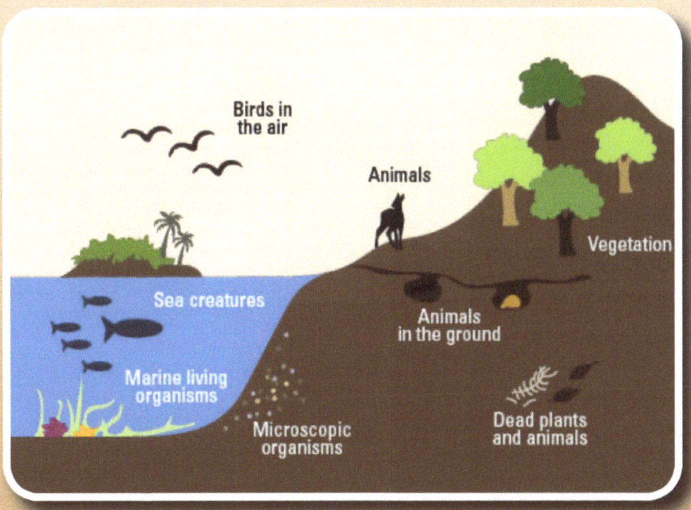

WOW!DOMAINS ARE SO EASY TO UNDERSTAND NOW.

I promise to keep the earth
clean and green.